"The best designers sometimes disregard the principles of design. When they do so, however, there is usually some compensating merit attained at the cost of the violation. Unless you are certain of doing as well, it is best to abide by the principles."

-Lidwell, Holden & Butler. *Universal Principles of Design*. Paraphrasing William Strunk Jr.

An attractive style is created by flaunting the rules. To flaunt the rules, you must first know them. This book is written to give a brief introduction to some of the most basic rules of lighting for Film, TV and video production. As a student advances, they learn which rules can be bent and which rules can be broken, but they always remember that the rules exist because they provide consistent results in the ideal situation.

Contents

Introduction

There are two factors that contribute to capturing and image with a camera: the camera and the lighting.

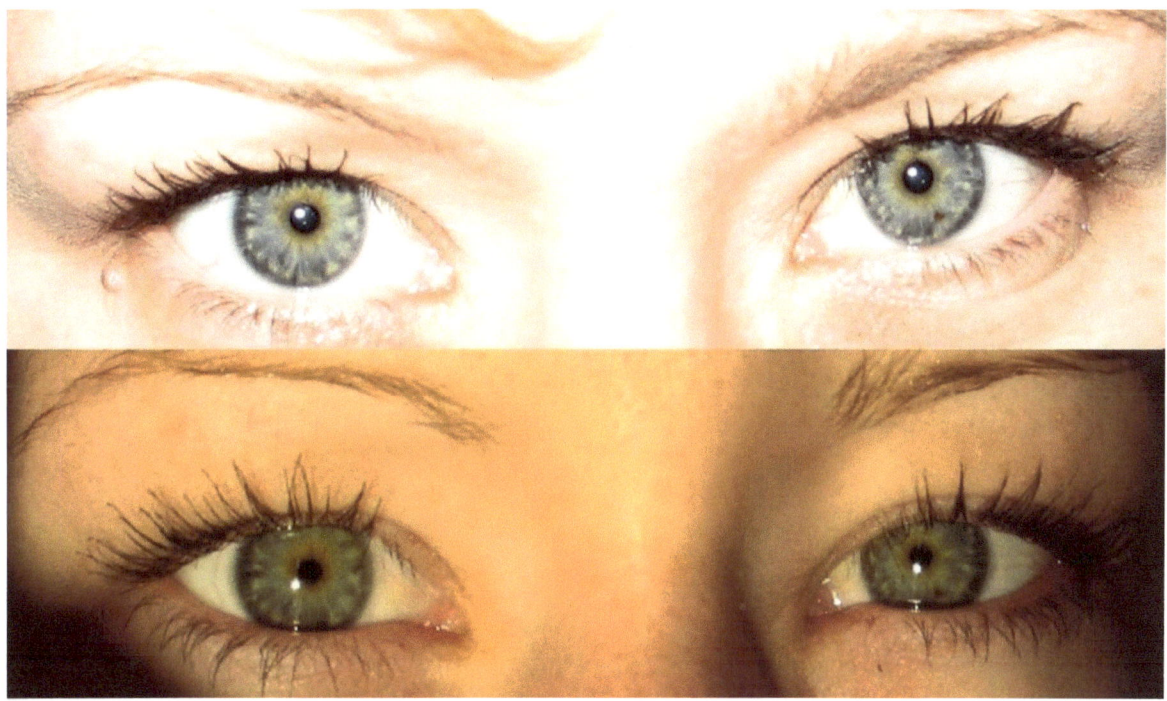

Most modern consumer cameras are capable of producing high quality images in most situations if the subject is lit properly. Professionals use cameras that are more versatile, allowing them to handle the tricky situations. For the majority of scenarios, using proper lighting will have more noticeable results than using a more advanced camera.

The best images are made when everything is brightly lit with good use of lighting and shadow. If this isn't possibly, make sure that everything is equally bright. This second option is often referred to as flooding the set with light or 'flat' lighting. Lastly, the poorest images are captured when no attention is paid to the lighting.

Properties of Light

Hard Light/Soft Light

Light is made of rays that travel in straight lines.

Light is considered 'hard' when all the rays are pointed in the same direction and are parallel to one another.
Hard light creates shadows with very distinct edges and a hard transition between light and dark.

Light is considered 'soft' when the rays are less ordered and instead of travelling parallel to one another, they are at different angles.
Soft light creates gradual edges and a soft transition between light and dark.

Hard light can be 'softened' by reflecting the light off a surface or by using translucent materials to diffuse the light. Soft light can never be 'hardened'.

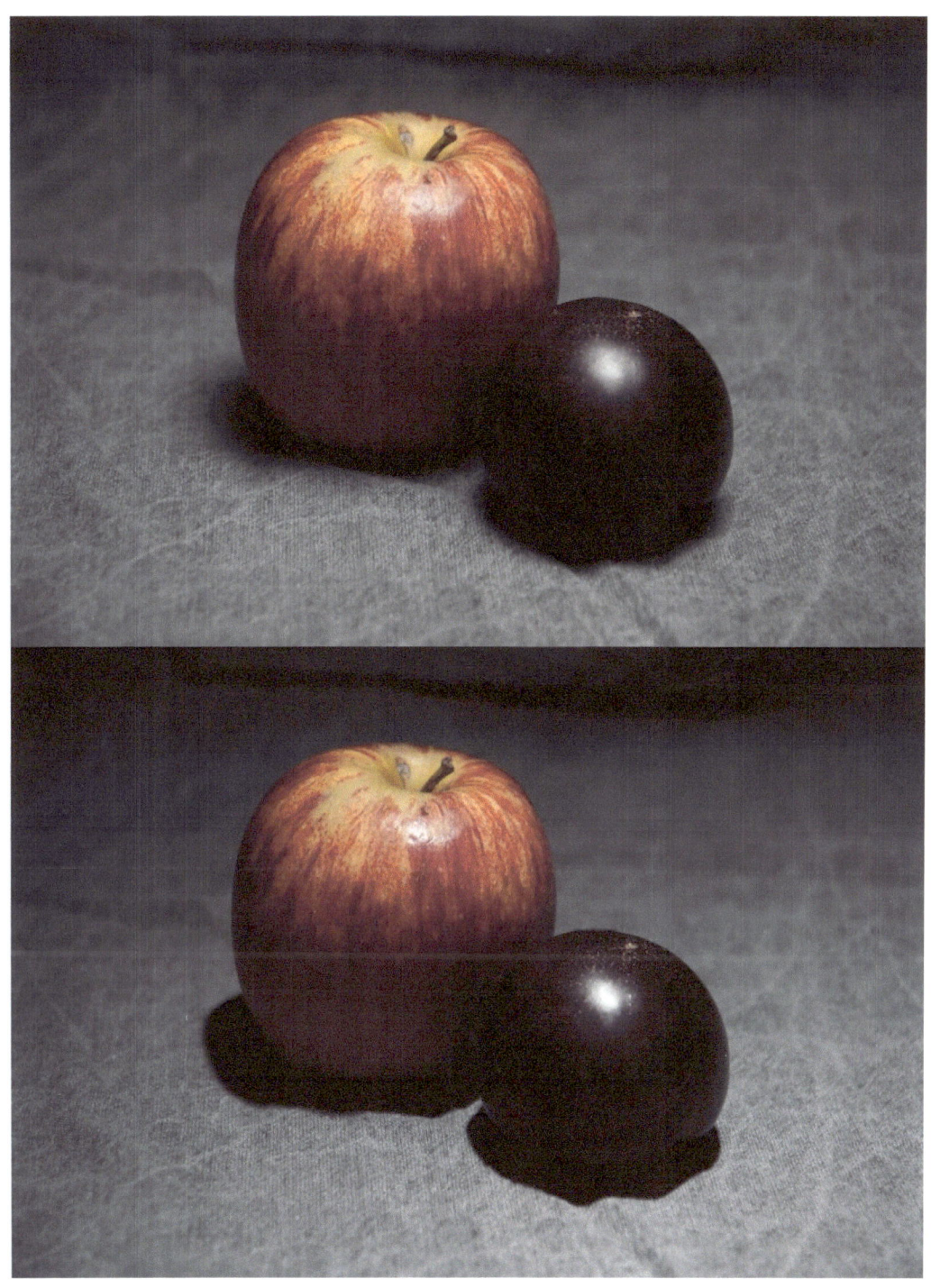

Example of soft light (top) and hard light (below). Notice the difference in the edge of the shadow.

Colour Balance

White light isn't always the same white. This is more evident in buildings that have a combination of incandescent tungsten and fluorescent lights.

Colour Temperature is measured in Kelvins (K) and is related to the physical phenomenon of black body radiation. When a body of matter that is opaque and non-reflective is held at a constant uniform temperature it glows, emitting electromagnetic radiation at a specific spectrum and intensity depending on the temperature. Kelvins are the standard international unit of temperature. Bodies at 1,000K glow a reddish hue and hotter objects progress through orange, yellow and eventually blue hues.

Daylight can vary from 5,000-6,500K, depending on the time of day and cloud cover. Lights and cameras are made to have daylight set to an arbitrary figure, usually around 5,600K.

Many studio lights use tungsten bulbs which have a colour temperature of about 3,200K.

Compared to daylight, tungsten lights appear redder

Fluorescent lights traditionally have a colour temperature of about 5,000K. With the shift towards compact fluorescent bulbs for domestic use, many manufacturers have made compact fluorescent bulbs that are balanced to around 3,200K, to mimic the tungsten light that is more familiar to people at home.

Compared to tungsten lights, fluorescent lights and daylight appear bluer

There are filters ("gels") that can be placed over lights that change the colour temperature of a light from tungsten to daylight (CTB) and from daylight to tungsten (CTO)

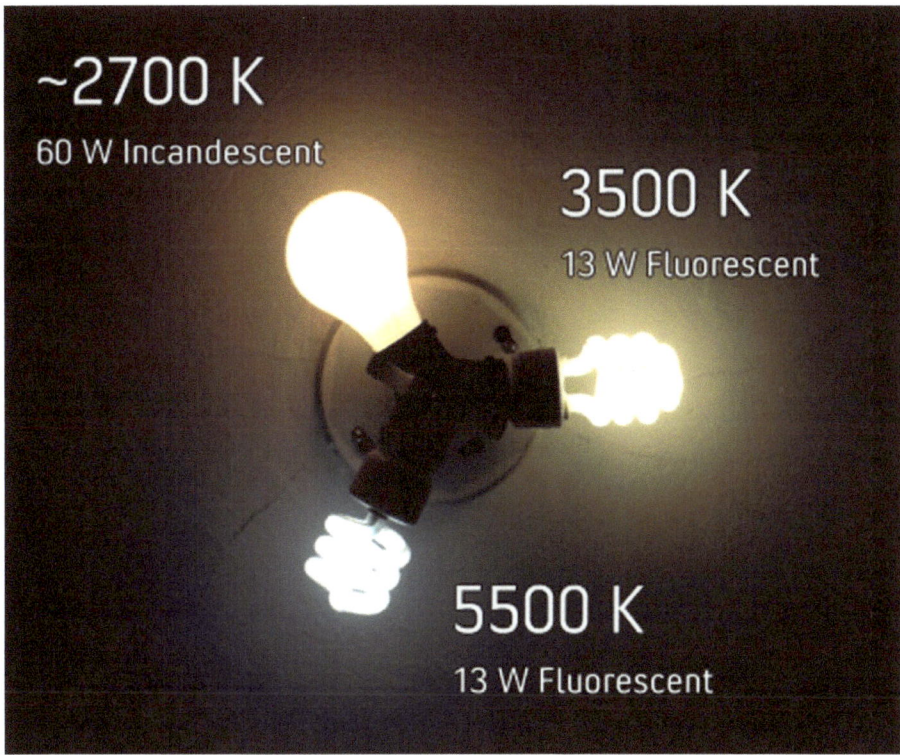

Cameras have to be *white balanced* to designate which light is 'white'. Most consumer cameras do this automatically finding the average or basing the selection on the 'most likely' white object in the scene.

High end consumer cameras and professional models allow the user to manually *white balance* by either selecting a preset level (daylight, tungsten or fluorescent) or arbitrating a certain colour as 'white'.

Above is an image where the camera was balanced to daylight. As a result, the 5,500K light appears the most white, while the others of lower colour temperature appear redder.

If the image was taken with the camera being *white balanced* to tungsten (~3,200K). Then the 3,500K fluorescent coil would appear the whitest, the 60W incandescent bulb would appear only slightly red and the 5,500K coil would appear bluer.

The best images are made when light with different colour temperatures are used in coordination with each other to create warmer or cooler images. The second option is to make sure that every light used is the same colour temperature.

Film Lights

Here are some of the more traditional options for lighting in the Film and TV industry. LED lighting technology is entering the market as an option that is more energy efficient, allows for variable colour temperatures and is more resilient to mishandling. LED lighting units vary with manufacturer and model but the principles are the same.

Red Head Lights

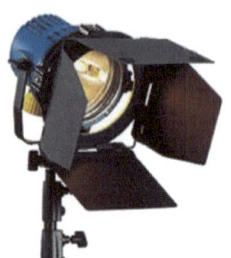

Red Head is a generic term to describe a range of lights that share two main qualities:

1. They can adjust between spot and flood
2. They typically use an 800W tungsten halogen globe

The example pictured here is an Arrilite 800w open-face focusing tungsten floodlight. The beam is focused using the yellow control at the back — this adjusts the reflector rather than the lamp, which should give the lamp a longer life because it is not being moved.

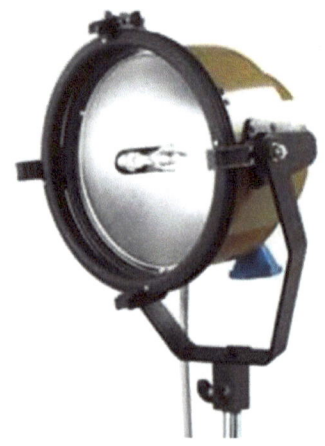

Blonde Lights

Blondes are typically bigger, brighter redheads. Power rating can be 1000 to 2000 watts, although the term generally refers to a 2000w open-face unit.

HMI Lights

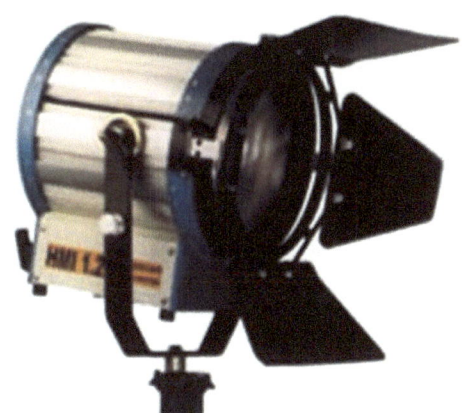

HMI (Hydrargyrum Medium-Arc Iodide) is a type of light which uses an arc lamp instead of an incandescent bulb to produce light.

HMI lights require a *ballast*, an electronic (or magnetic) device which provides the ignition pulse and regulates the arc. Being 2 to 5 times as efficient more efficient than incandescent lamps, HMIs use less power to produce the same light and run cooler. They are also balanced to 5600K, the same as daylight. This makes daylight shooting easier, because you don't need to use gels.

Halogen Work Lamp

Halogen work lamps can be purchased from most hardware stores. They are a cheap alternative to specifically designed industry lights, however are often used with industry equipment for additional effects.

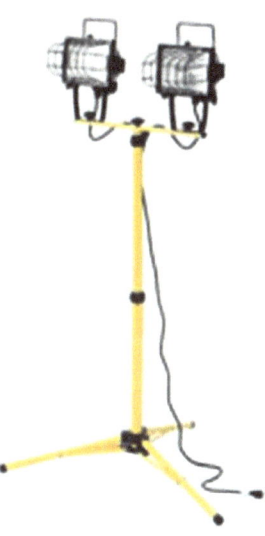

They can be used as primary lights, but compensations must be made as you would need to use more lights and will have issues with multiple shadows.

When in doubt, you can use lots of these to just flood the set with light.

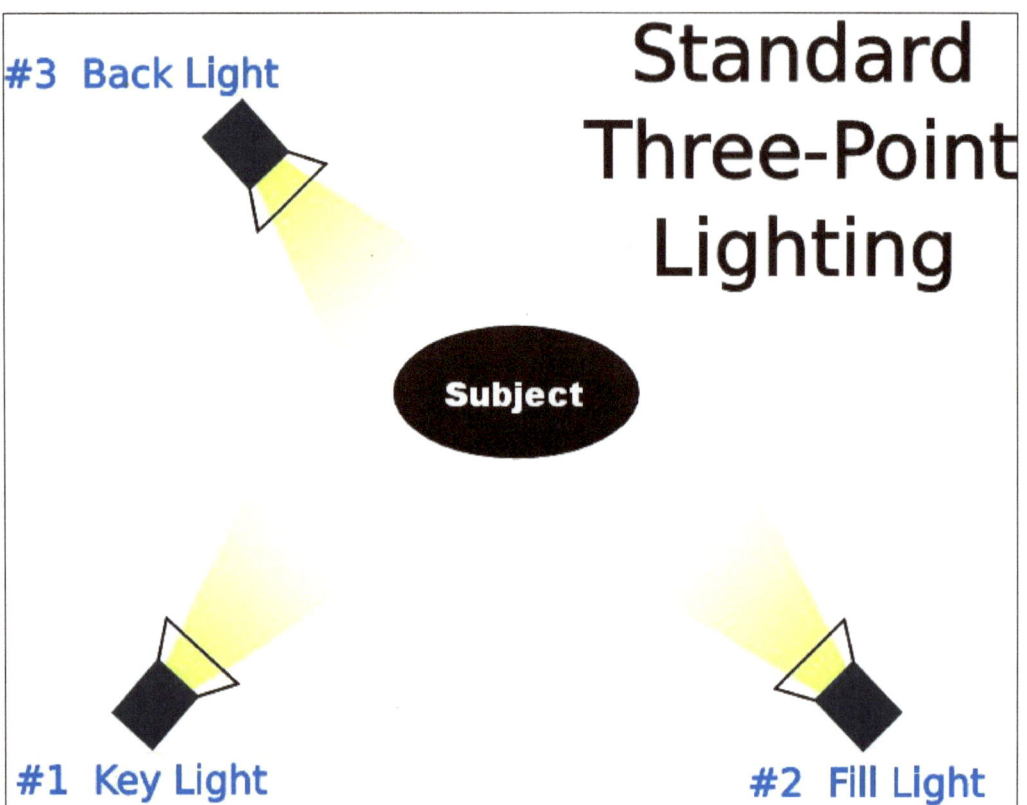

The standard 'ideal' lighting arrangement is three point lighting.

It begins with a Key Light which is the hardest light and brightest on the subject.

The second light is the Fill Light, which is a soft light that is used to 'fill' the strong shadows cast by the Key Light and to raise the overall light levels.

The third light is the Back Light which functions to visually separate the subject from the background by creating a subtle glow around the edges of the subject.

A better image can be achieved when the lighting levels of the background can be controlled by background lights. By controlling how everything in the scene is lit, the Director of Photography can create an image that fully utilises all the fundamental design elements and principles to create an image that achieves the desired effect on the viewer.

One of the key effects is creating the illusion of depth, which helps focuses and direct the audience's attention, creating a more engaging and interesting image.

Intermediate concepts

Natural Light

When shooting indoors and there is natural light on the set, you have three options.

- Block out the light with whatever is available, practical and safe.
- Overpower the light with artificial light.
- Integrate the natural light into the scene, keeping in mind colour temperature.

These options are listed in no particular order. The decision is usually made based on practicality of the situation.

Bouncing

Light can be bounced off a surface to function as a Fill or Back light. A similar result can be achieved by using a reflector or just polystyrene board.

If you can't place a fill light effectively in the scene because it will be in-frame or there is no electricity, consider using a reflector to bounce the ambient light back on the subject or positioning a light so that it will throw light on the ceiling and reflect down on the subject.

Outdoors

If you're filming outdoors, during the day, then the sun will most likely be the brightest, hardest light available. Without a significant lighting rig, the sun will become by default, your Key Light or your Back Light and all other lighting must work around it.

When filming outdoors, all the lights and cameras should be balanced to daylight.
Reflectors are very useful for outdoors shooting as substitutes for Fill Lights.

Sharing

A single light can be used for two purposes. In an interview situation with two subjects, diffuser can be cleverly used on only half of the light so that if can perform as both the Key Light on one of the subjects and the Fill Light on the other. Depending on placement of the subjects, Back Lights can double as Key Lights and Key Lights can double as Background lights.

Shadows

The introduction stated that:

"The best images are made when everything is brightly lit with good use of lighting and shadow. If this isn't possibly, make sure that everything is equally bright. This second option is often referred to as flooding the set with light or 'flat' lighting. Lastly, the poorest images are captured when no attention is paid to the lighting."

Shadows add depth and emotion to the image. These are two elements that make a more engaging image.

It is, in order of preference, that:

1. Shadows are well used
2. Shadows are eliminated
3. Shadows are badly used

Audiences are more accepting of having no shadows in a scene than having bad shadows.

Depth

Photography and Film, like painting, is set in a two dimensional medium. Creating the illusion of depth always adds a wow factor and can be used to direct the viewers' attention.

Appendix 1: Depth Perception

Binocular Cues

Retinal Disparity

With the resurgence of 3D movies, this is the most commonly known technique in creating the illusion of depth. Your eyes are in different places and so receive different images. Our brains compare the differences and use that comparison as a reference for depth.

The image below is a stereogram. When viewed at the correct disatance, the imags will overlap and it will appear as one 3D image. A stereoscope will assist in viewing this image.

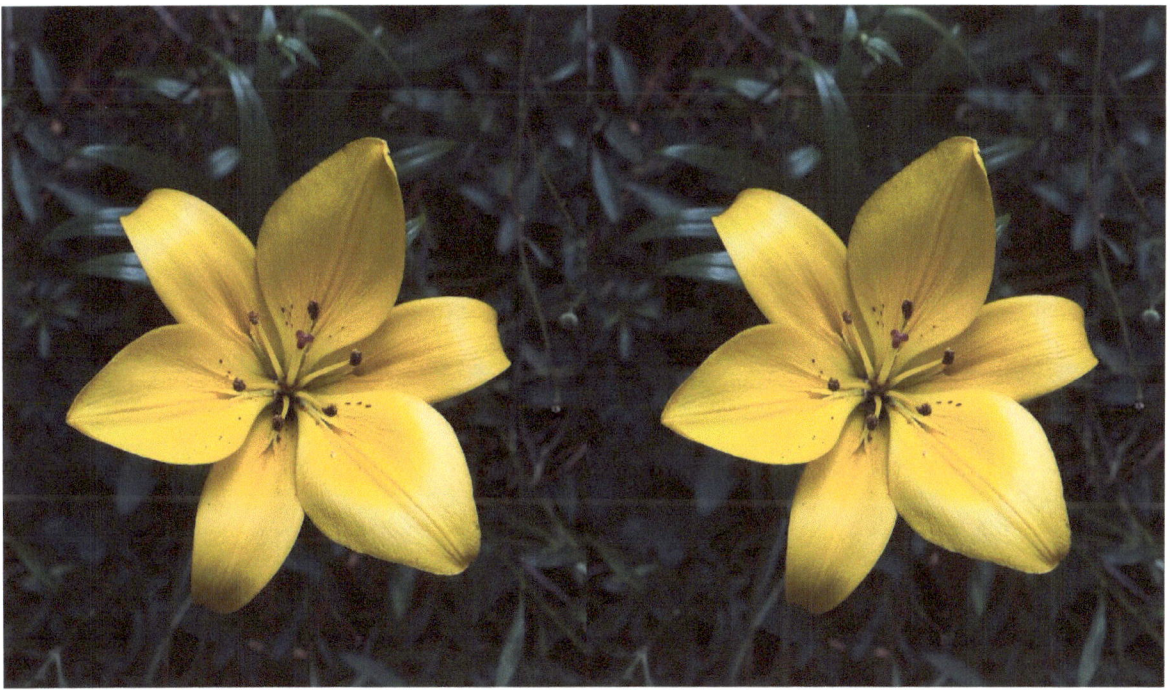

Convergence

To focus on an object that is close (such as the tip of your nose) our eyes need to rotate inwards, potentially until we are cross-eyed. For objects that are further away, our eyes are pointing almost straight forward.

Monocular Cues

Relative Size

When we see two objects that we assume to be of similar size (such as two people) the one that appears larger is interpreted to be closer.

Interposition

If one object blocks our view of another, we assume that it is in front.

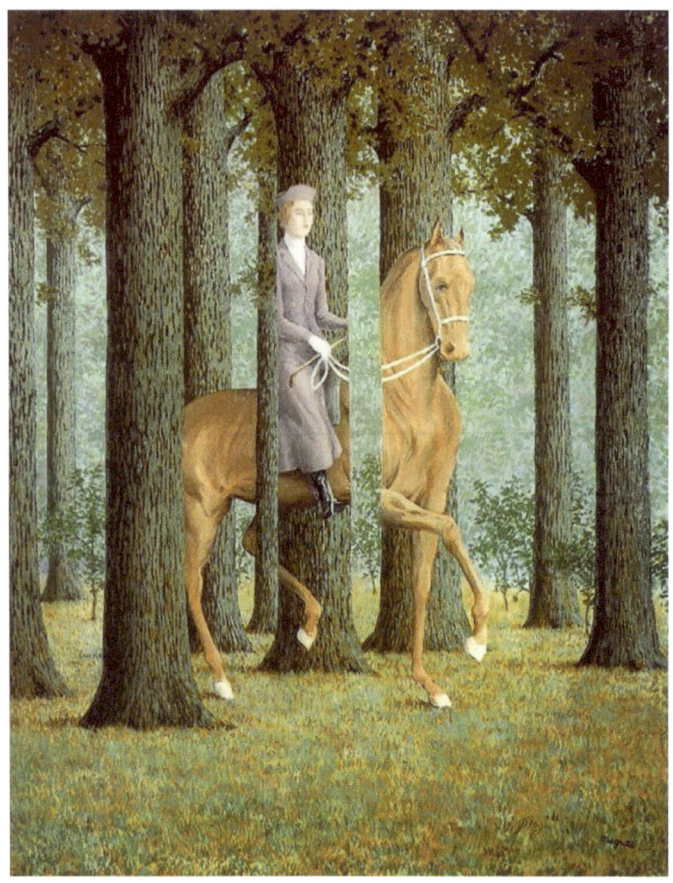

René Magritte, *The Blank Signature,* 1965, National Gallery of Art, Washington DC

Relative Clarity

"Fuzzy" objects appear further than "sharper", clearer objects. This is noticeable when people try to judge distances in fog, mist or rain.

Texture Gradient

Objects that are further away appear smaller and tightly clustered compared to closer objects. The image below, uses texture gradient and linear perspective in the buildings in the background to create depth.

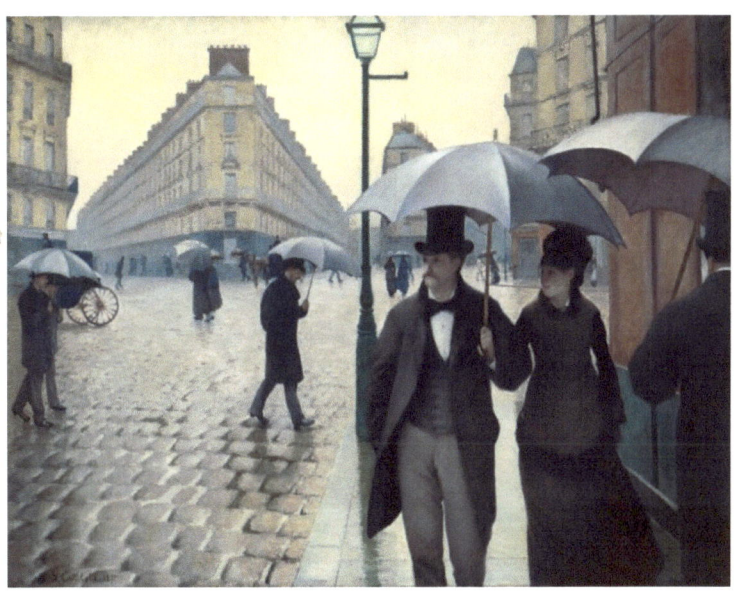

Gustave Caillebotte. *Paris Street, Rainy Day*, 1877, Art Institute of Chicago

Relative Motion

When an observer moves, the apparent relative motion of several stationary objects against a background gives hints about their relative distance. If information about the direction and velocity of movement is known, motion parallax can provide absolute depth information. This effect can be seen clearly when driving in a car. Nearby things pass quickly, while far off objects appear stationary.

Linear Perspective

Parallel lines appear to converge as the distance from the observer increases.

Light and Shadow

Closer objects reflect more light than further objects. Thus brighter objects appear closer. This can be achieved through the object being more reflective or being better lit.

When an object casts a shadow on another, we assume that it is in front. This relates to the cue of interposition.

Phillips - McIntosh
Produce | Promote | Profit

Phillips McIntosh exist to support and retain the creative community of Perth, Western Australia. Our focus is the Film and TV industry, where our process is simply Produce, Promote, Profit.

Film and Video *production* involves more than just a professional crew. To be ready for production, a concept must have undergone an appropriate amount of preparation, which includes strategy, refinement, writing and research.

When *promoting* content, Phillips McIntosh aim to innovate uses for the 'new media' platforms. By strategically creating content that people want to share and by positioning that content to be found easily by the intended audience, we can create viewership and direct that attention to where you need it to be.

Profit to be sustainable. We help businesses through creating content that promotes their brand and improves their web presence. We also utilise international distribution structures such as Amazon and iTunes to directly benefit off content that the public have deemed valuable enough to buy.

You can find this booklet, the DVD of our seminars and other content at *shop.phillipsmcintosh.com*

Keep in touch with us at *www.phillipsmcintosh.com*

ISBN-13: 978-1470114442

ISBN-10: 1470114445

www.ingramcontent.com/pod-product-compliance
Lightning Source LLC
Chambersburg PA
CBHW041310180526
45172CB00003B/1048